BOA
EDITIONS LTD

TROUBLE THE WATER

Winner, 2015 A. Poulin, Jr. Poetry Prize

Selected by Mary Szybist

TROUBLE THE WATER

POEMS BY

DERRICK AUSTIN

FOREWORD BY MARY SZYBIST

A. POULIN, JR. NEW POETS OF AMERICA SERIES, NO. 38

BOA Editions, Ltd. ⫯ Rochester, NY ⫯ 2016

First Edition
16 17 18 19 7 6 5 4 3 2 1

For information about permission to reuse any material from this book please contact The
Permissions Company at www.permissionscompany.com or e-mail permdude@eclipse.net.

Publications by BOA Editions, Ltd.—a not-for-profit corporation
under section 501 (c) (3) of the United States Internal Revenue
Code—are made possible with funds from a variety of sources,
including public funds from the Literature Program of the **ART WORKS.**
National Endowment for the Arts; the New York State Council on
the Arts, a state agency; and the County of Monroe, NY. Private
funding sources include the Lannan Foundation for support of the
Lannan Translations Selection Series; the Max and Marian Farash
Charitable Foundation; the Mary S. Mulligan Charitable Trust;
the Rochester Area Community Foundation; the Steeple-Jack
Fund; the Ames-Amzalak Memorial Trust in memory of Henry Ames, Semon Amzalak,
and Dan Amzalak; and contributions from many individuals nationwide. See Colophon
on page 96 for special individual acknowledgments.

Cover Design: Sandy Knight
Cover Art: *10-79* by Diedrick Brackens
Interior Design and Composition: Richard Foerster
Manufacturing: Versa Press, Inc.
BOA Logo: Mirko

Library of Congress Cataloging-in-Publication Data

Names: Austin, Derrick, 1989– author.
Title: Trouble the water : poems / by Derrick Austin ; foreword by Mary
    Szybist.
Description: First edition. | Rochester, NY : BOA Editions Ltd., 2016. |
    Series: A. Poulin, Jr. New Poets of America ; 38
Identifiers: LCCN 2015046377 | ISBN 9781942683049 (paperback)
Subjects: | BISAC: POETRY / American / African American. | POETRY /
    Inspirational & Religious. | SOCIAL SCIENCE / Discrimination & Race
    Relations.
Classification: LCC PS3601.U857 T76 2016 | DDC 811/.6—dc23 LC record available
at http://lccn.loc.gov/2015046377

BOA Editions, Ltd.
250 North Goodman Street, Suite 306
Rochester, NY 14607
www.boaeditions.org
A. Poulin, Jr., Founder (1938–1996)

for my parents: Derrick and Tracy

Contents

"Summertime"   61
Deepwater   62
Apology   63
Persian Blue   64
Dominion   66
Jezebel   68
Cedars of Lebanon   69
Blue   71
Canaan   72
Dead Gull   73

Sleeping Alone   77
St. Mathew's Pentecostal Church   78
Primer for Sainthood   80
Sweet Talk   81
Magnolia   82
Sweet Boys   84
Visiting Mount Calvary Cemetery   85
At the Grave of Zora Neale Hurston   86
Vespers   87

Notes   *89*
Acknowledgments   *91*
About the Author   *93*
Colophon   *96*

Foreword

The tonal complexity of Derrick Austin's remarkable debut begins with its title. "Trouble the Water" is, of course, a phrase from the spiritual "Wade in the Water."

> Wade in the water.
> Wade in the water, children,
> Wade in the water.
> God's a-going to trouble the water.

It is a sorrow song married to a vision of great hope and faith, conjuring the Exodus story of God parting the sea to allow the Israelites to escape enslavement in Egypt. Whether we hear the final line of this refrain as a promise of deliverance or a threat might depend on the group (the Israelites or the Egyptians) with which we identify.

The refrain also echoes the story of Jesus healing the sick and afflicted told in the Gospel of John, which serves as epigraph to this collection. In both the Hebrew and Christian testaments, water—and more precisely, moving water—is the element one must enter to be saved. This spiritual is said to have been used to instruct those trying to escape slavery: wade in water, and the dogs attempting to track you will lose your scent.

In all these scenarios, spiritual salvation is not imagined apart from physical salvation. The life of the body matters deeply in this collection, and the life of the body unfolds in a world in which not all bodies and desires are equally valued and protected. Austin never loses sight of the realities of social injustice and environmental trauma. His startlingly innovative "Blaxploitation"—a sestina in which every line ends with "black"—begins:

> Another night of "I'm not usually into black
> guys but . . ." and I'm alone with Johnnie Walker Black
> and too many movies. I'm not offended. No black
> moods at all. . . .

The humor and heartbreak simultaneously at play is characteristic of Austin. He knows how easily individuals and particulars fade into labels and received narratives. "[Y]ou tell me the story in which I mistake you for the story," admits the speaker of "Persian Blue." This is what Austin works to resist. In his poems, human experience is always embodied experience. The spiritual and the erotic are inextricable. In a world where we habitually "ghost past each other," Austin's speakers investigate the experience of relating with enormous attentiveness and care. His speakers imagine what it might mean for them—with their particular bodies and desires—to wade into what will transform and heal. These poems inhabit a multitude of spaces: churches, bedrooms, cemeteries, museums, gardens, catacombs. There is a lounge, a nude beach, a hurricane party, a "picnic in a field of goldenrod and trumpet-flower" just "[o]utside the old city walls." A deep knowledge of history, myth, and art is at play throughout these imaginings, but they always come back to the body and make us feel how often we touch each other "by not knowing how."

In the Bible stories from both Exodus and John's Gospel, it is not human power that troubles the water, but divine power. In using the shortened phrase "Trouble the Water," Austin moves his title away from a report of what God will do or what God's angel did. The title is a command, one that Austin seems to have given himself in writing this book. In *The Marriage of Heaven and Hell*, William Blake warns, "Expect poison from the standing water." These poems come to "trouble" the still waters of old assumptions, to unsettle and renew. "Primer for Sainthood" ends:

> What wouldn't you pay
> for an endless night with the god? O you
> who would starve for such music,
> there is another sweetness saved for those
> who wash and bind the wounds, who join the feast.

This is a book of that other music, that other sweetness. Austin reminds us that the power to trouble does not belong to God alone. The title's injunction to "trouble" is for all of us, but Austin's poems show us how it is done, show us how it can be done. In "Cathedral," when he describes a Christ figure who has "been brought down from the cross again, / as in the Gospels, for restoration . . . ," he is also describing the work of his own poems. The speaker of "The Catacombs of San

Callisto" reflects:

> We're told by books old as these walls:
>
> Filthy, our bodies, yours and mine. Not so.
> When we love, we take each other in
> like living water until warm
>
> plaits of air unbraid in our throats.

These poems are so alive, so good, so full of wit and charm and sorrow and tenderness and grace, I feel like one of the Sunshine Lounge listeners in "Torch Song," mesmerized by a singer who is "singing slow tonight, feathers swishing / like the hair of a riled hound." Austin's poems have all the strange electric power of his singer's song. "Listen, baby," the singer knows, "when I open my arms to the crowd and mouth / the night's first note, I don't sing; you singe."

—Mary Szybist

For an angel went down at a certain season into the pool, and troubled the water: whosoever then first after the troubling of the water stepped in was made whole of whatsoever disease he had.

And a certain man was there, which had an infirmity thirty and eight years.

When Jesus saw him lie, and knew that he had been now a long time in that case, he saith unto him, Wilt thou be made whole?

—John 5:4-6

Tidewater Psalm

. . . in heaven it is always Autumn
—John Donne, Christmas Sermon, 1624

By sunset, the crickets' trilling begins
in the airless damp, rich with salt
and the sulfurous fumes the Gulf flags off.
Bristling cattails brush my hands.
The light-crested water rises and falls
like a chest flecked with blonde hairs.
I feel estranged from You.
A shoal of minnows breaks, silvering
my ankles, like a mirror; my heart swims
in gladness at the changeable world.
Tell me in heaven it's warm enough to wade
into this fine transparence, never want for air,
only light and water, and be as the river
flowing into the sea which gives up its name.

Devotions

All night you pace between our bed and another
room in the house, fetching glasses of water
when you mean shots of gin. The candle
doesn't catch your naked body—a leg, the cut
of stubble—only the shadow of its leaving,
the whole of you uncontainable like the moon,
its kissable face and its darker chambers.

Mary offers her mangled son, a matchmaker,
from the dollar-store votive by the bed.
(Other nights John the Baptist rolls his eyes at me.)
You're the one who stayed, or
at least never left. You stay because of hard rain,
or dead magnolia on the drive; or is it custom
for the wounded to care for the wounded?

Where are you? I need a solitary room
with you in it. Wall me in. Lie down on me.

Okaloosa

I like the heron best
        because it has no song,
flying over the water, its mating

cry mournful, aggressive, and internal.
        Seaweed and creamy foam

float on the tide's restless lapping,
licking my feet like a lost dog.
      I am no master.

The Gulf collects its own scraps:
        rows of hotels
hollowed out and plastered
ochre by sunsets, knocked down by Ivan   *Hurricane?*
or Dennis—you lose track

after so many seasons.
        Mist hangs over shoddy condos.
Beachcombers scan the quartz burrows
of ghost shrimp. A drunken couple
stumbles somewhere. Before they were expelled
Choctaw called this place *Okalusa,*
      "dark water."

The land and the body
       are complicit in their own decay.   *— what does this mean*
Our works turn spindrift in the sea.

A heron lands on a brick and will not move
        as I walk past, its beak
a crusted ancient weapon.

What am I to it
                    but another animal
competing for dunes and fish?

The great blue flies off. Calling, calling
its mate. Even with walnut brains they understand.

What is it

Pass-A-Grille

I look for you on the storm-smoothed shore,
        glittering where the moon tows itself
across the bay. Cool air fills my lungs with mint

as I walk past sea oats, past sea grapes
        in tidal pools. Waves spread
like playing cards—a flush the land can't beat—

and the sea keeps upping the ante: first,
        quartz and chrysolite, then breakwaters
and wooden weirs, then the land itself,

an erosion so ceaseless I too want to give
        my body, wholly, to something else.
Camped by a fire, you call to me.

The sea shuffles its indifferences, the way
        desire moves in us, wearing us down,
indifferent to the one who offers himself—   *indifferent to sacrifice*

rows, swims, coasts, or floats
        face down. The lighthouse
winks its one good eye. The hull of a tank ship rusts.

Mouth to mouth, we're our own drowning.
        And if we're found,
your skin will be blue linen over my body.

you cover me

Breakwater

In the photograph, my grandfather stands
      in sepia water off Mont Saint-Michel,
barely older than I, having chased wine

and women. Fresh from the Italian Campaign,
      swaggering on the shore,
he points at his brother beyond the frame

(killed a year later by cops who mistook him
      for another black man)
watching lambs whose salty meat is prized

So nonchalant

in Normandy, whole racks for christenings.
      You could taste the tide, he says.
Which means what exactly? That he could taste

the salt of stones or the salt of tears
      from those seeking St. Michael's blessing,
before the water's shift, its sudden gallop?

As a kid, he taught me the tide's faces
      on morning fishing trips,
the Gulf eroding the bricked-up present,

gray light opening over emerald waters
      like the camera flash that froze him
in France—one of the few things fixed

in his afflicted mind. When the nurse
      carries in his meal, she takes me
in the hall, asks if his memory's holding.

I shake my head. When it started to go he said,
     Most days it's like hearing Marvin Gaye
being shot, the same news over and over,

and I never know if I'm Marvin or his father.
     I take him to the park for an afternoon.
He skips rocks on the river's opaque surface.

Once there was nothing here but water—
     an argument with no winner; a row
of sandbags to reproach the building waves—

where the North Star line rusts on tracks,
     where his wheelchair idles beside me.
The Gulf will wash and sweep us into silence

where grief cuts like breakwaters.
     I don't claim to understand anything—
whether all this will turn into salt or waves

of light containing what we've lost or forgotten,
     where Technicolor flowers spring
and spray the air with oils. For now

the dark river laps the white, bristling heads
     of clover where my grandfather stands
by a peacock when its green-gold tail flashes.

Torch Song

They call me Ma'am here, in The Sunshine Lounge,
the daddies and twinks weary even in the beginning
of their lives. They call me Lena, after Dietrich

and Horne, of course, their Blue Angel,
their Black Piece of Ass when beer's cheap.
Take a seat. Unbutton your collar. Buy us a drink.

I'm singing slow tonight, feathers swishing
like the hair of a riled hound. Like my gown?
I pricked my finger so many times sewing these

gold sequins. I'm a star. They call me Southern
Cross, and they know what they like. They take
long swigs from longnecks. I'm pierced.

That's where the light shines through. I'm less than
woman and more than man, light rocketing off
my body, wig a dollop of blonde. Listen, baby:

when I open my arms to the crowd and mouth
the night's first note, I don't sing; you singe.

Blaxploitation

Another night of "I'm not usually into black
guys but . . ." and I'm alone with Johnnie Walker Black
and too many movies. I'm not offended. No black
moods at all. I'll watch *The Seventh Seal*. Black
chess pieces slaying white, live or die, Bergman's black-
est phase. See I'm not mad. But if I were Black

Death right now, I'd slaughter Love. Fade to black.
Brides-to-be would roll around in ash, black-
en their dresses and veils in rivers black
as tar: Gather your roses, dye them red to black.
Then they'd hear the gallop. Metal no black-
smith could forge, flaming, sparking the black

hooves of four horses—red, green, black,
and white. *Who's that? Hallelu!* A miracle! Black
skies part and resurrected Love blacks
my eyes and rubs me out beneath his black
sole. No more pain. I'm better. Fade to black.
Bergman's done. I need magic. I call a trick. It's black

and white—he's red all over. *I love my black
boys sore.* He can't grip my hair, black
brillo pad. My body? Let's get physical. Black-
body principle, I'm light and afterglow. Black-
out. *Give me that nigger dick.* His bootblack,
I gave all of him a shining. Shocked a black

man took that? I've heard his shit before: black
's an absence, no stimulation for the eye's black
pupil, but I'm right here, still whole (Black
don't crack), and he (Once you go black . . .)
got off just fine. Sleepless, we debate watching a black
comedy or a foreign flick. How about *Black*

Orpheus? On the news, another case of black
on black. Where's the white on black?
The tone on tone? No nuance here? The screen black-
ens, then stutters over an ad for *Black
Narcissus* (Coming soon to Blu-ray . . .). Blue-black
night hems into dawn. I'm feeling Blax-

ploitation. How about *Coffy*? I am black
but beautiful, razor blades all up in my hair. Black
power. He touches me by not knowing how.

Bow Down

Let's talk of graves, of worms, and . . . what then—
are we that silent moment on the stage
when kings are out of rules and fools of puns?
Remember crossing the bridges by the sea,
you a stranger here, asking
the name of the tree ruffled with purple?

～～

It was knowledge, a kind of lording
over another, as when, sunning at a pool,
you dipped one leg in the water.
As if you were given all its crowns.

～～

Before you drifted into my life—
waiting in the wings—I said no to so much.
Nudging me, you said, *Please*
put it in your mouth. You do this to me.

～～

Kings wait to see who will kneel.
I've forgotten my line. Is this when I
abdicate the throne or bruise you
with my scepter?
                    I beg
your pardon. I would resign the crown
a thousand times to kneel at your feet.
What kind of king am I? I'm just as lost as you.

～～

Drifter, stardust, little marsh-light,
you are known by so many names:
Bassanio, Gaveston . . .

                             Try a new skin:
friar, courtier, dominance,
submission—it's all foreplay, role-play.
We bow. The curtain falls. Another night.

Major Arcana: Judgment

During hurricane parties, beer
      foaming on the curb,
        we prepare for the inevitable

return of glass-bottom boats,
      trawl nets, and oil cans—
        all we've cast into the water.

Jade oak leaves quiver
      and clouds wing
        from the bay. It's not unfamiliar

to see bodies in the water
      after flash floods. Clothed
        in tuxes and paisley dresses,

it's as if they'd brazenly decided
      to swim. If you stared
        long enough they would stand

tall and flat like the horizon's
      oil rigs. Instead they rest
        in slick loam

beside bricks and shattered cedar,
      dreaming of moss
        on cypress knees.

We're Standing on the Sun

you say when I break the aloe leaf
and smear its sweet, clear gel over your body.

On the nude beach, you get hard
and stretch skyward like an unfurling touch-me-not.

You dive into froth, nearly impenetrable,
maybe the shadows

of a few darting fish. I mirror you above,
twin planets, untouched and indivisible,

borne along by our bodies <u>toward a farther shore.</u>

Catacombs of San Callisto

He's never Himself in the earliest frescoes:
the shepherd boy guarding the sallow lamb
whose fleece might hide the god. Or the fish

and bowl of loaves. Or the phoenix.
He isn't Himself, yet I trust Him.
I've walked alone with a man in the dark

and made much of his body—
you're with me now, touring the nests of the dead.
We're told by books old as these walls:

Filthy, our bodies, yours and mine. Not so.
When we love, we take each other in
like living water until warm

plaits of air unbraid in our throats.
The early artists did not turn up their noses
to flesh and, in this way, honored

the putrefying bodies in their midst
and painted the signs by which their bodies
would be watched and known.

Long since emptied, the pocked tufa
is stained by old blood and filth.
I would gladly shame myself in this way for you.

I would be the good shepherd
above your body in its cold, stone niche
not only because I believe

in the resurrection of the body, but because
I want to be the face that welcomes you
to that inordinate dark.

Sans Souci

without care/worry

Sanssouci Palace
Potsdam, Germany

1. Caravaggio's *The Incredulity of St. Thomas*

We saw for a moment
laid out among us the body
of the complete human we failed

to be. What field did
the disciple pass
to encounter Him who

double-crossed all
boundaries? Green-white tufts
of angelica

crushed
beneath His toes—dusty
from the tomb—

scent the air,
the smell of a world in which
nothing rots or grows putrid.

Cruel body, which gathers and leaves
such sweetness.
Only darkness in the painting,

the body's inmost color.

2.

I believe in art more often than your cock.
We thought a getaway would loosen us up,
shake off our post-Freudian feelings.
We should work on us, I say. (Sorry,
I'm an ice queen.) You light a Turkish cigarette,
its smoke not so different from the incense
in the nearby church housing a saint's
gilded hand—if not flesh, then body be gold.
Can't you just suck me off? (I'm alive.)
Sometimes drinking beer together, chilling
the sweat on our chests, is enough.
You lean against the French door,
all the hairs of your body black and glistening.
I turn to minutiae and away from you.

3. Anthony van Dyck's *Pentecost*

<u>Tongue</u>
alight tongue aloft <u>tongue</u> inspired
eyes look up

tongue in darkness
<u>tongue</u> flickers
a whipstitch

bolt
of lightning binds
sudden clouds <u>tongue</u> debased

oyster <u>tongue</u>
tucked between palates
not satisfied

flame-tipped
like the disciples' hair and black
beards

lapis <u>tongue</u> chalk tongue lead
<u>tongue</u> renews
twice burned <u>tongue</u>

coaxes honey from stone

4.

We ghost past each other this morning,
after a long evening of wine, without
reproach or welcome, like the day-long
rain locking us in. It sweeps the roof
with repetitive strokes. We take for granted—
we are so accustomed to these bodies.
You lick your lips, brush my unshaven cheek,
and say, *You look at me like a painting*
you think you know all the names for,
while I'm bobbing between your legs.
Have you ever seen yourself please another?
Our reflections live silently in the French door pane
between lightning strikes, a kind of pleasure,
refining their gestures in another room.

5. Etching of Adam and Eve

It's not
in any of the stories—
 you'd have to use your imagination

anyway—this cave scene lit
 from within,   .
  light like Rembrandt's—

light of the mind, light
 of fireflies in heat.
The luminous dark is etched

like stone after centuries of ice
  and water, those clasped bodies
   indistinguishable

from mossy crags
and the stream, molten
 in its brightness,

breaking above them.
 *Lean in. The painter said
  they're dying.*

I think they're gathering food.

6.

Slowly eat out my asshole, slowly while bees
lave daffodils on our balcony and remember
each bloom with dance. You growl. I lick
your armpits. *Come, come for me*, you say,
our moans made fluid on our canvas of a bed.
Travel makes one adventurous. To know
and glory in our bodies' torque and bristle.
We ran from His body in the gallery,
afraid, aching to be sore. There was no halo
in the painting, but there's a cock ring here.
You teach me what the Old Masters can't—
the crimson flush running over you already
fading into memory—yours are the hands
that master and finish me with a final stroke.

Illumination

Witness the monk
          tracing figures
     on bright, empty pages.
Shine and color rise

      like mist
     in meticulous outlines,
his path illumined by
      a dribbling candle.

     Wanton overgrowth,
spiraling arabesques,
       the works of his
     hands blossom

on both pages: split pomegranates
       (cinnabar pigment,
     iron rich), a lattice
of jade leaves (lapis worth more than

      a year's wages)
     and rose gold shocks
of bougainvillea. His garden
      is the centerpiece.

     Hares and falcons
and the gentle flick of
       his brush,
     white for a hind's tail;

cows graze flat fields (perspective
       as yet unknown).
     And all these are named,
as when Adam reared and ranked

      their tribes,
     for a prince's solitary pleasure,

each beast and blossom.
                    Every page gilded

        as if to pollinate
those fingertips. And this
            is but one page, one page
in a book of praise.

The monk inks the owner's likeness
                    in a green cloak
            lined with gold leaf
to echo the landscape

                (the body politic
        easy parable for a boy). But this garden
is very real. See there,
            how the monk

        bearded and wiry, inserts himself
and points to the adjacent page?
                    A flaming sword.
            Two figures

evicted from their green shade.
                    The vellum
            supple as with her tears.
Both cover their nakedness

            with a banner,
        he holds the word *humus*
and she, *hubris*.
                    Written

        on the flesh.
The ash and soot of a
                book burning
            just under her foot

as if ruin made our shadows.

St. Sebastian's Executioner

A stag chews waist-high grass under an elm.
Its herd sleeps, each a bright, wet weed,
in a freshly rain-swept field turning in the wind,

flashing dark then bright like a soldier's skin—
my bronze arm paling into my shoulder's moon.
Wind brushes the stag and me. It is cool

and touched by mint. I draw the bowstring.
It jerks its large, brown head. A black bear
lumbers out of underbrush, a drunk, dizzy

and bright with honey. No. Bright with bees.
Like memory or apprehensions of the soul,
they anchor their needles. The bear stops.

Numb and swollen, swollen, too, with sweetness.
Is my soul like the bear? Or the stag and its cud?
Or the cud after being flushed through its body?

Or the bees at their wax and gold palace, guarding
a sweetness they cannot consume but will die for?
Like me, he was a soldier, bright clay-colored beard.

He was not young with his belly and puffy limbs.
He was not quiet any more than he was beautiful,
tethered and beaten, but I still cannot name what

he died for. His death was many years ago.
I am the bear trudging off—bees gone; herd moving,
unmoved—to whatever mean peace it knows

in the wet woods. Like the strain of a bowstring,
bow's blowback, faith separated in me
as he looked at us, the crust of sky. Stag or criminal,

sign or saint, I will spend my life flying toward you.

Byzantine Gold

A chain of blue-white chips mimics waves
                    pleating
          around Christ's body. Owl-eyed saints

draw light on the western wall.
                    Despite
          centuries of votive smoke,

the shining ranks of prophets gesture,
                    elegant
          as sommeliers, toward mosaic scrolls

and would have you consider the honeycombed
                    geometry
          of paradise—dome, arch, and column—

with its air of permanence,
                    above penitent
          and tourist, above the fray

of ethnic cleansing we'd like to believe:
                    a Balkan
          land mine planted near trillium,

the scarred field, the ghost limbs of olive trees,
                    and the boy
          there, I mean, he's a man now,

about my age, passing us on his prosthetic leg—
                    that which was
          sundered brilliantly shining—though

he might have been a child when he lost the limb.
                    Think invention.

Think miracle. To think someone, Doctors

OH my God?

Without Borders, maybe, could make a man whole again.
        But look:
    a mortar leveled Gethsemane,

Visigoths defaced the deposition, and,
        her turquoise
    hem unraveling, poor Mary's going to pieces,

pocked by shrapnel from a mislaid bomb.
        If the dome
    cracked open, what a dry comb it would be.

We consider paradise anew despite its stone
        indifference
    to time. *Christ Pantocrator*, alien, severe,

claims the apse, suspended in gold
        leaf, apart
    from and a part of the world, the dust

those semiprecious stones become. We would find
        comfort
    in his Renaissance flesh,

its bordello-shades of pain—the oils
        of the canvas
    like the oils of the body—but where

would we find warmth beneath these glass eyes,
        radiant,
    petrifying? His gaze arrests us

like everything we make, which is touched
        with our image:
    metals and mirroring glass

in mortal shapes, even the minefield,
                    visionary
            in its violence—God before Sodom

would be amazed by such force. The mind
                    itself
            drips rough honey and gilds the world.

O-P-U-L-E-N-C-E

Great wealth or luxuriousness [handwritten]

*O-P-U-L-E-N-C-E. Opulence. You own everything. Everything
is yours.*
                    —Junior LaBeija, *Paris Is Burning*

I've sashayed into your life from another time.
              Silk ascot and oxfords
        as I take a turn around the garden.

        I'm dolled in lace and whalebone
corset, crying in a mirrored hall.
        There's no sweeter sound than the opera of indulgence. /

              A waltz? I've whirled with Mozart.
Why watch countesses when the ballroom is up the block? /
        Let's vogue and duckwalk. Our bodies barked into motion.
        House music slinks and shivers.

        [My soul is velvet, sovereign, black.]

Princess Sisi's bright salon, her plaited hair is damp with tears.
              Pissing from a gondola. The Gardens of Bomarzo.
Just off Ibiza, Armand De Brignac fills our cups.
              McQueen. Met Gala. The ambience of coffee
when you hate it. Tilda Swinton's cheekbones. The abs
        on Cristo della Minerva. Legendary Leiomy Mizrahi.

        Opulence is felt and heard. It's darling.

        Darling, come away with me.
Darling, lick the sugar cube
        inside my mouth.

        Darling, dust the chandelier.
Darling, read your Henry James. Darling, gossip ruins lives.

Darling, bend. Darling, leather.
Darling, can you tell a life? Darling, do you have a self?

You deserve it, darling.
Darling, read your history.
⌊Darling, call me sir.⌋

City of Rivers

City of Rivers

All this—the bridges, the market, epitaphs—
were under silt not long before we came
to the city that marks its years by rising floods.
As we pass a shop on stained stone streets,
a glassblower fashions an urn from fire and air.
Lace-makers scrub rust from a door's agitated joints.
This is the city, someone said, *you never enter into
the same way.* I wanted this passage for us, abandonment
and remaking, the cicada stripping itself from itself.
Despite peach iced tea, the heat sticks to us like flies.
Even the plaster walls of our rented room sweat.
Where we going tomorrow, you ask, emerging, naked,
from a cool shower. Rivulets chart your body's cartography;
they steam and shine and lift themselves to you.

Crown Glass

Scrolling through our photos—
you under amethyst and garnet windows—

silence crosses my heart
as when ripples in a pond flutter and part.

You look like a stranger,
blind gaze, a bust drawn from water.

I've never seen you more clearly.
The chapel was almost empty

when you pulled me outside:
past tourists, their flustered guide,

and a stained-glass St. George.
Wings of sweat stain our shirts. A forge

puffs smoke; a glassworker mixes silica
with potash, lead, and soda:

cathedral glass requires flaws.
Like love or faith, self-sabotage

goes a long way here.
Light scintillates and disappears.

Something said, *What illusions do you crave?*
It was not the city but the waves.

Whose promises do I
hear from a distant bridge? What lies

have we heard or told
under cathedral glass and stolen gold?

Fountain Statue

A god breathes through the lips of anyone
loved by an artist
She is rendered in marble   fallible
like memory   And water
spurting from a dolphin's muzzle
erodes her hair   the tangled bounty
of a fisherman's haul   razor clam
spider crab   squid   cuttlefish

Rain   as we and dozens of musty
tourists pass her   It is not
mercy   merely the sky
flinging its gorgeous indifference
for when all travel has ceased
the ruined fountain gurgling with the illusion
of life   who will remember
the girl   let alone the god

Effigy Without a Body

Rest after restlessness and your body
like moonlight on the river, wavering.
Outside, bells and tugboat horns
keep me up. Night's brackish river-
scent as your body; fragments of a foreign
tongue looping into song:
                              Where are we . . .
how do we . . . how much . . . may I touch?
Earlier, in a little chapel, among effigies
of kings and bishops, you touched the
broken chest of king's favorite, Moorish,
a singer of Provençal. They were lovers
or they weren't.
                      One man letting another
in as if out of the cold raised suspicions.
When the king died, a small mob's hammers
pelted the stone face and crossed arms
like rain. They burned the royal pepper trees.
Like a troubadour song, the scent lingered
after the hammers and flames hushed.

Antaeus

When thirteenth-century ships from Greece
      bearing caskets of perfumed oils
arrived at dawn, sailors thought the city floated
      above the earth and sea, like a gem,
the light skittish on it, surface and depth blurring.
      I close the brief history book
on the velvet bookmark you bought me
      and watch the evening news. An anchor
recounts daily life on a new Atlantis.
      What business is it of ours? We're passing through,
you say, reclining in translucent linen pants.
      We wrestle; it begins as play, of course.
Bear hug. Laughter. Lifted up like Antaeus,
      I'm powerless before you.
Another night suspended between heaven and earth.

Cathedral

He's been brought down from the cross again,
    as in the Gospels, for restoration:
    limestone Christ, entombment scene,
        soon cleaned of mold and grime,
the divine enfleshed in dust, the flesh of time.
    If I were a finer believer, I wouldn't see
    His body in immodest repose,
        the Classical physique, as I see you
undressed by moonlight and want to rest against the stone.
    But unlike Him you keep me warm. Look,
    He's been brought down before—ancient graffiti—
        and had *love* carved into Him once more.

The Bait

Fishermen in motorboats poised
on anxious waves talk in bursts,
        breakers against wooden weirs.
One yanks up a sallow cod. I imagine myself
as that fish with the rictus of a mouth
        like a puppet, expressing innocence
and stupidity, lunging for the bait (worm twisting
        into hook), drawn into the fiery clarity
of oxygen (my dying must be like a mosaic),
chilled and sold (the pans of a scale; words like gulls
        above me), gutted, exposing all
the simple gemlike gears of my erotic life (your kindness,
        drawing me out of myself, is not a knife
entirely). Before your lips, I passed through many hands.

Little Gospels

Outside the old city walls,
       we picnic in a field of goldenrod and trumpet-flower:
Cabernet and fresh bread to sop olive oil.
            Wind runs its hand through uncut leaves.
You lick spilled wine from my chin,
       whisper something I lose to the wind. I've imagined
little gospels, so many ways you could leave—
            I play dead like a rabbit in a falcon's grip,
numb but for the talons in its hair.

Ghost Slipper

Before merchant ships were bound to the harbor
by closed trade routes, they traveled east
with spring's warm wind
for lapis lazuli, azurite, and indigo.
To acquire devil's blue, painters crushed the stones
and mixed the powder with linseed oil.
Eastern goods were lost, so they used charred wood
to blacken the skins of demons
and render the flesh of Berbers, Moors, and Africans.

The oldest fresco in the city depicts the Queen of Sheba
received by Solomon and twelve jeweled retainers.
Though, in the story, he will be abandoned,
it is she who remains. His throne
faded in a flood, his pale pigments didn't last a century.
Her hands, delicate as sparrows, gesture toward the ghost
of his slipper. She still loves what failed.

Conveyance

The city's song outlasts us.
Not church bells or the grumbling truss

bridge or the hawker's
cry but currents conveying a chorus of travelers.

The city is suspended like a damselfly,
lifespan as long as its glassine wings. I

can't take any of it with me.
The city might not last the century—

greenhouse gases, government pawns—
already the portraits and relics, even your bronze

hands settle in memory's murk. Who
will meet me on the other side? If not you,

then water.

No Union

Like a sluiceway, the church door opens
and the wedding party tumbles all their joy outside.
Bridesmaids, bells hemmed to their gowns
like drops of light on wavelets, invite friend and stranger
to the wedding feast. Who would not be swept away?
In a wide courtyard—ribbons and amber-
colored columns—hours unspool their gold lengths.

Nightfall. Candles. Wineglass after wineglass
leads me down my heart's marsh grass,
a will-o'-the-wisp. Bitterness swats my face
like moss and ivy's elegant nooses. Forgive me.
I'd been alone so long, and I'm trying
to keep it together, like Frankenstein's bride
who, scrapped together, was built for bribe.

Heaven and Earth

Rain connects heaven and earth.
The colorless city shines outside our window,
distant marble domes like fresh snow.
Water pours from every *duomo*,
their gargoyles' sputter song. Rivers tow
boats into annulling fog, aimless, slow.
We tarry here. In the *Commedia* a soul said, *O*
pilgrim, we are citizens of one true city. Go.

Rain connects heaven and earth.
Never own more than you can carry, locals know.
Bloom and shed like an apple bough.
I know this and have nothing to show
for it like stone seraphs at their ledgers. None blow
horns to call us to an end. Let's drink Bordeaux
tonight darling, shamelessly, below
the angels' eyes and make them blush: speak low.

Rain connects heaven and earth.
The rivers, stained as if by wine, are indigo.
Flashes stain the skyline's smooth tableau.
Lightning's nimble fingers thread a bow
into the ombré sky and then will sew
new stars into the hem or maybe throw
it all away—how easily bodies blow
apart, warp and weft, wake and undertow.

Pin me. Mend me. We've
got so far to go. These are the lessons I cleave
to in this city, which weaves
and unweaves, weaves and unweaves.

"Summertime"

A pipe burst somewhere. The record kept turning
Porgy and Bess. Granddad sang the old blues tune.
I told him my name. The water was burning

when we went to the coast, green and churning
like collards in the kitchen. It was June.
A pipe burst somewhere. The record kept turning.

He took worm-colored pills at ten in the morning,
sometimes he wandered off. I'd find him at noon,
streets away, calling my name. Water was burning

from Gulf Breeze to Grand Isle, the Gulf swirling
like vinyl. Egrets blackened the bayou.
A pipe burst somewhere. The record kept turning

when we watched the news in the nursing
home: men in white scanned the dunes.
I told him my name, that the water was burning.

He looked through my eyes and sang *fish are jumpin'* . . .
I said his name, washed his feet, left the room.
A pipe burst somewhere. The record kept turning.
I told him my name. The water was burning.

Deepwater

Grand Isle, LA

White crosses speckle a sun-baked route.
>They count those that cannot count themselves:
>>mirliton vines like feather boas

on fences and lean trees; pompano, grouper,
>rosy spoonbills; amberjack, spadefish, diamond-
>>backed water snakes.

The highway runs to the coast's stained
>brocade, warning flags watch over drums
>>of Corexit. A gust

whips up the nervous laughter of yellow tape.
>A swaybacked pier gathers gulfweed
>>and tar balls as the tide

>rushes in with the stink of nitrates and oil.
>>Come, take chrism from these waters.

Apology

Because I was not hungry

I ate your apricot: because I'm a beast,
not craving flesh just the dark, gnarled pit:

because these are all the shards on the floor

and the one unbreakable glass:
because you told me not to

I gobbled whole globes, soft

bites whispering *off, and off, and off*
until I unbuckled my belt to fit myself:

because I wanted you to catch me,

throttle me, and take my fingers in your mouth:
because it hurt to breathe

those colors, its skin all fire and earth:
because the fruit was firm,

the flat of your palm,

against my cheek: because bruised
skin spares no tongue its sugar—

Persian Blue

Tampa Museum

1.

We leave the jewels and daggers, a long wool rug
        whose dyes have deepened to rust—
you don't notice. Near the exit, two guards chat
        about the spill. A sea-blue bowl
dazzles me, its craquelure like arteries, blue ink
        where blood would be. No one
knows the name of the woman in the porcelain,
        offering a man sweet cakes.
Could she be Scheherazade, each night always the first,
        cushions unchanged, pastries never stale?
They've been buried centuries, no one to complete the story.

Is it still that dark underwater, the guards ask?
        You tell them of the dead zones, cloudy-
eyed fish covered in sores and scars; of fishermen,
        their nets slack with fewer crawfish and oysters.

I come when you call, swept away from the bowl,
        full of unfulfillment, and down terraced steps.
In the park by the riverwalk, children dodge jets of water,
        their joyful noise sharp as crystals.
The brown Hillsborough River flows into the bay
        and circles the dozens of spoil islands.

2.

Tonight, our thousand and second night,
tell me the story of our laughter
through sudden summer rain.

Tell me the story of salt: on your shoulder,
chest, and chin. Tell me how that first week
we seemed to know our pasts by heart,

where we'd been and where we planned to go.
Tell me the story of how we woke up wet
in each other's arms and watched the Gulf

widen into deep water where, beyond our vision,
an explosion claimed eleven workers,
smoke billowing skyward, a dark reflection

of the darkness below. Who's to blame?
Who knew what? We can't keep any story straight.

3.
Somewhere the Gulf still rolls brightly ashore—
          after oily booms were hauled in,
dispersants and matted wings, "Closed for Business"
          and wringing hands, and thousands
of small fish, pale as plaster dust. On that shore
          crabs shuffle out at night and mate.

We watch gulls float down the old river, vanishing
          under a bridge. Plastic bottles idle
in bilge, until an unseen current carries them away—
          the way we'll part.
                                        Across the river
the university gleams, its confection of bricks and minarets
          like gingerbread with icing dusted silver.
Perhaps, Scheherazade's bowl—its story inked into bone
          and china clay—would fill for us with wine.
We would trade it between our lips and see the picture
          rise with every sip while our faces warm
and you tell me the story in which I mistake you for the story.

Dominion

I know your works:
        netting palm-sized oysters
and crabs, stinging them
        with cayenne and lemon.
                You bulldoze water-logged
foundations and sheet metal rusting in intersections,
                                building, rebuilding,
so you and the hurricanes you name
        like children have somewhere to go.
                Marsh grass parts
for oil drums. Your sons and cousins work
        the rigs, an aunt sweeps
                a gift shop
painted with cartoon swordfish and shrimp.
        What would you do otherwise?
                But I have this against you:
subsurface plumes
        and lesioned fish belly up in booms.
Men in hazmat and business suits
                roped off the coast
and authority was given to them over me.
They said: *The spill will clear,*
        neither will there be tar balls
                nor dispersants. These will be washed away.

        I miss your boats docked
breast up on cypress knees,
        the trawl nets
                combing over me. I miss
reading their names reflected backwards.
        I miss pelicans and swimmers.
Despite my name,
        what you leave to the delta I collect.
                I ring five horizons, like sleep.

When algal bloom and nitrates lap
                       your feet, when crawfish
spill onto your plate, I
        am at your table.

Jezebel

Where dusk's last minutes collected
along the curves of Tanqueray bottles,
mosquitos swerved having had their fill
of gin-flushed blood. I nursed a longneck
by the cooler, catfish on ice jeweled
with flies. You were slick and coffin-sharp.
You promised to make it snow in May,
which reminds me—too late—of Borges
on love and fallible gods. I believed
the world crystallized for you.
Snow collected on the crown of my head.
No. You flicked cigarette ashes on me.
Touch me, touch me. O hounds of memory!
All night gnawing and lapping my palms.

Cedars of Lebanon

*His legs are as pillars of marble, set upon sockets of fine gold: his
countenance is as Lebanon, excellent as the cedars.*
—Song of Songs 5:15

If you can see them, the snow-covered
cedars, crowning the hills, come

to the cabin between the two tallest,
their branches hooked

with the tantrums of crows.

~~

Will you find me without the pink and blue hydrangeas?

Will you find me without the spikes of St. Augustine grass?

Will you find me with the bloodied snow—where some frail thing was

raptured?

~~

If you find a stag and kill it,

throw its hind legs over your shoulder
and drag it to my cabin
between the tallest cedars.

Its blood on the snow is my voice pursuing you.

~~

I sleep on a cedar bed
with red fur blankets,

the wood of the gates of paradise,
wood which hid the naked couple.

Wood of shame. Wood of passage.

If you come, I'll press my hand
to your chest. A key

to the fittings of a lock.

~~

You knock at the door.
Break several cedar branches

and dust off the snow.
Bring in seven for the bedroom,

seven for the fireplace,
then rest your head on my chest—

even bare
branches can make a kind of summer.

Blue

Derek Jarman, 1993

We watch his final film in a small, dark room,
which is his body, lit the color of blood
before being blushed by oxygen. His chorus of friends
and muses, like a bowl of delphinium petals.

Handfuls of nightshade-colored pills, a nurse's
cold stockings shuttling between the sick,
the dying, and the last, men who've loved men.
He was shocked into a new body each morning:
blindness, more lesions, less function in a limb.

His soul tarries here. We hear the waves
he heard outside Prospect Cottage, shuffling
sea wrack and driftwood. Blue is his beloved's arms,
cradling cornflower, hydrangea, and heliotrope
from their garden, radiant blooms passed on to us.

Canaan

See the figs and citrus groves, beehives
like noisy bangles. A couple gathers
oranges, brushing away white blossoms.
Egrets preen on the riverbank.

You would bask here forever.
Move toward them. So little divides you,
those quiet birds, and buckets of fruit
from the water. If only the river could forget

the land: pickups, houses, picnic tables
hurricanes cover and carry away.
From the other bank look back
through haze brooding over the river,

ambiguous as oil burning off the coast,
at windward trees bent east, where you are going.

Dead Gull

Little Icarus who once stole spit
from your father's mouth,
stole life wherever you could, you did
not deserve this chemical bed,
oil gummed to your wings.
Worms tunnel through your body:
blood, water, salt, flesh
distilled into base elements—
everything you are is useful to everything else—
a transformation
I envy.

Sleeping Alone

Consider the moths throwing themselves into lampposts,
knocking the threshold of light: consider the fireflies'

green glow, clear as human need: consider the shining
poppies: consider the ghosts of his hands on the mirror:

as each light goes out, consider he, too, will sleep alone:
consider how these arms are empty in bed and know

when darkness presses a poppy's soft, pink folds,
it's not absence, for once, just another coupling.

St. Mathew's Pentecostal Church

The choir sways, mouths wide with air and light.
In the back pew, I stand and clap beside a man
with years of Jim Crow etched into his face.
I've never seen someone so intent on listening.
His cane on the pew, he stands and sings,
a credo when you've lived long in this country.

Chariots whisk our troubles to God's country.
Sister Jones's hat, trimmed with light
blue flowers, shakes when she rises and sings
a different song. She moves past the old man
and me, trembling, muttering, listening
to her own invisible rows of black faces.

She looks to the ceiling, then falls out. His face
sweaty, the old man says, *She actin' country.*
Girl ain't got no damn sense. We listen
to her speak in tongues, half a language of light,
half Patti LaBelle. *I'm going to meet the man,*
going to meet him down by the water, she sings.

To see himself crowned in light, a boy sings
like Sister Jones. His mother pops his face.
The crowd applauds and cheers. Some men
sigh. Seen too much in Alabama's countryside.
A stained glass cross, like blue fire, lights
a ring around our congregation listening

to one woman's spectacle. No point listening.
Who says the Lord bears white roses and song?
Expect a fire to the heart. He will press His light
into our bones and mouths, wear out our simple faces.
Bless the fool who enters the Lord's country
expecting Him to love like any man.

Bless us who have known the touch of man
where it's lifted and dropped us. Bless us listening
to spirituals mocked in King Cotton's country.
Bless us who shake and sob without a song.
When we wait by the twisted cedar and face
the river, dappled with light,

a stone inside our guts called *light*,
and listen to a lark sing another country,
looking for the Man's face—bless us.

Primer for Sainthood

So you want to kiss the passionflowers
in his hands, the blooming flies and blood?
So you would fast and serve his meals,
meats and bread, liquors, sweets?
Happily, you say, drunk on the waters
of his smile. And if he does not smile
that day? If out of boredom he says, *Kneel
and wash my feet, every day you must
drink of this water.* Happily, you say. Again
with this happiness. And if he breaks you?
Batters you with his fists? Batters you
like a door and hands back your happiness
—a dozen knocked teeth—would you say
Again my lord? What wouldn't you pay
for an endless night with the god? O you
who would starve for such music,
there is another sweetness saved for those
who wash and bind the wounds, who join the feast.

Sweet Talk

after Kara Walker's A Subtlety, or The Marvelous Sugar Baby

And how would you tell them from me?
Am I solid, good sirs? Do I melt? You gentlemen
have such excellent taste. It would take you
days to tread me out. Lash me with your tongue.
Would you know me then? I want to know.

Concrete beats sugar from my soles, tar-black
tether of my footsteps. The children of cane,
bodies too much of a good thing. In another life,
their smiles would gild cathedrals. In another,
I would never say *In another life.*

They are like altar boys and the bells they ring.
What music do you hear? *We are precious as ambergris.*
We are precious as oil and crowns
of gold teeth. Gentlemen, am I valuable? Would you
touch me and lose your touch in me?

I am not light-skinned (*I am dark, but comely*)
nor am I light-skinned like these boys,
luscious with the sun. Can you see us now? Are we still
anonymous as bones on rum-colored velvet?
This much I can tell you: I have been skinned

by the moon; my flesh is a loitering man—
collar unbuttoned, beckoning—near the alley
where he takes you, you and my flesh
opening like a book, and the night gains new knowledge—
Oh, my body? Were you gentlemen interested in that too?

Magnolia

Rows of church windows, five-
          pronged, milky with light,
are like magnolia blossoms—though

they are like lilies, too, and cotton also—
but they're most like magnolias
          I sat under in late summer,

watching their wax goblets and shuddering,
          chiaroscuro leaves seem to
          turn and flutter like fans:

a row of dark limbs shot through with white,
a procession of women whispering or softly crying
          but they were a cluster of trees, and I
          imagine while I looked

one carnivore ate of another and each other and one,
          perhaps, escaped into the brush,
into survival, which is, after all, an admission:

I will be attacked again—though the killing
                    between animals is not a sickness
          in the soul, but who am I to say, I did not
                    see them, and I do not know.

A man once said I was lovely like those flowers, but I am not
          in the least like the petals, more
like the rough stamens and carpels, a black head
on snow, like the heads of Saint Maurice and his decimated brothers,
          the trees shaggy with Maurices,
silent heads nodding in a perfumed field, not unlike
the heads of the congregants, all our heads

under magnolia-shaped windows. I can't stand to
look ahead
at another dead black boy.

Sweet Boys

after Kara Walker's A Subtlety, or The Marvelous Sugar Baby

define this temple of erasure and refinement.
Sweet boys like tropic flowers, machetes, and blood-sweat.
Sweet boys and their archaic smiles. Pursed lips
like the leaves of an unopened book. Sweet boys shock
the antebellum night like ghost trees blanched by salt.
Sweet boys, the Southern Gothic swaying in your dreams
to make your sleep easy, their bodies now magical—
burning, dismembered, singing—to make the myth
easy. Take a picture. Sweet boys consider the daily minstrelsy:
white men throwing signs and smiling for photos,
their grins like flesh wounds, and there, the white woman
assessing the sphinx's ass and genitals. Photo. Photo. Photo.
Sweet boys think, *This is what it is to be a nigger.* A language
of locusts and honey in your mouths, a poultice of resin
in the mouths of the dead. Sweet boys like jawbreakers.
Sweet boys balloon with fire. Sweet boys chase each other through
a burning mansion, and you all merely marvel at the light.

Visiting Mount Calvary Cemetery

*If I had my way, I'd have been a killer. I would have had guns
and I would have gone to the South and given them violence for
violence, shotgun for shotgun.*
—Nina Simone

Nobody knew her name, the murdered woman
found outside of town, black hands severed.

Nobody claimed her. Cypresses and willows
so thick they seem dark blue crown the hill

where white families have traced lineages,
clear as garlands on shimmering headstones.

Down here, where centuries of black bodies remain,
only one is named: Sophronie Davis (1855–1950).

All else is spiny undergrowth. Huge brush piles.
Even black churches lost touch. No one kneels

to scrub the graves free of bindweed and husks.
Some miles east, another black cemetery's gone

to sea. Fishermen cast lures from half-sunken graves.
If I have my way, there won't be fire next time

only water again, water crowning Mount Calvary.
The dead will stand amid the congregated waters,

their black bodies shimmering and loved, clothed
in gowns, names written in water and air and stone.

At the Grave of Zora Neale Hurston

I kept my mad hound, Zora.
We wandered many miles,
pollen and dust staining us
the gold of ancient idols.

I got wet dog under my fingers.
He smells like me now, too,
you see he's carried road kill
all the way here—raccoon,

then possum, hitched a fawn
five miles north, buried a fox
outside of town—it's in the blood
of his teeth. He found me, too,

by the roadside. Followed me
ever since. That first night,
I saw myself as that hound
licking my own face clean.

That morning, a distant cousin
gave me his gun, told me
to kill it. I couldn't shoot him.
Anything that loves you will

lay down for you or know enough
to fake it. I'm a coward in my life
unlike my work. I don't know
which is worse. So many things

are conspiring to kill me, Zora.
Not only sickness and guns
but the tongues of those who
would sooner kiss me or call me

lover. Zora, it's not my dying day.

Vespers

Lord in the pigment, the crushed, colored stones.
Lord in the carved marble chest. I turn away
from art. You are between my eye and what I see.
Forgive my errant gaze. Tonight, I can't sleep
and won't frighten the deer in my peonies.
Like children who rub their grimy hands over everything,
they only want to touch and be touched by grass.
They've never known violence, cars howling out of darkness.
Lord in the camellia, drifting in and out of sight,
like those blushing, perfumed heads will you welcome me?
I, too, am little more than a stranger in your garden.
Stroke my velvety antlers. Open your palms.

❧

Notes

"Blaxploitation" makes reference to Ingmar Bergman's film *The Seventh Seal*, Marcel Camus's *Black Orpheus*, Powell and Pressburger's *Black Narcissus*, and Jack Hill's *Coffy* starring the legendary Pam Grier. In physics, the black-body is an idealized physical body that absorbs all electromagnetic radiation.

"Bow Down" is titled after the Beyoncé track released March 2013. The first line partially quotes from a speech by King Richard in Act III, Scene II of Shakespeare's *Richard II*. Bassanio of Shakespeare's *The Merchant of Venice* and Gaveston of Christopher Marlowe's *Edward II* are both characters whose desires can be read as queer.

"Major Arcana: Judgment" is an ekphrastic poem after the tarot card. Symbolically, the card represents self-reflection, absolution, epiphany, and the need to make life-changing decisions.

The Catacombs of San Callisto, or the Catacombs of St. Calixtus, are among the largest in Rome as well as home to some of the earliest Christian art. The final two stanzas refer to the fresco of "The Good Shepherd" in the catacombs, one of the oldest representations of the figure.

Sanssouci was the rococo summer palace of Frederick the Great. Its name derives from the French phrase *sans souci*, from which the poem takes its name, meaning "carefree" or "without worries." Nowadays, the palace is a museum holding, among other treasures, Caravaggio's *The Incredulity of St. Thomas* and Anthony van Dyck's *Pentecost*. The etching referred to in the fifth section doesn't actually exist and is a bit of notional ekphrasis on my part. The first sentence of the poem also steals from Virginia Woolf's *The Waves*.

Contrary to most artistic depictions of Saint Sebastian, the earliest texts and images describe him not as a beautiful youth, but as a much older man, a former soldier in the Roman army.

"O-P-U-L-E-N-C-E" is titled after the quote by Junior LaBeija in the documentary *Paris Is Burning*. The film explores the ballroom culture of the early 90s populated largely by gay men and trans women of color.

The sequence "City of Rivers" is very loosely inspired by Venice. The reference to *The Divine Comedy* in "Heaven and Earth" paraphrases a line spoken by Sapia, a sinner on the terrace of envy in Canto XIII of the *Purgatorio*.

Many of the poems in the third section of the book directly respond to the Deepwater Horizon oil spill, one of the worst ecological disasters in American history. The entire Gulf Coast was affected from Texas to Florida. Containment methods included the use of booms, skimming, burning, as well as using the chemical Corexit which studies have shown is harmful to both marine and human life. Since the 2010 disaster there have been eighteen oil spills in the United States alone.

"Deepwater" is inspired by a photograph which appeared in *The New York Times* on June 17, 2010. The photo, taken by Nicholas Pechon, depicts "a lifestyle memorial set up along Highway 1 in Grand Isle," rows of white crosses in which the names of animals, foods, and cultural objects important to Louisiana are elegized.

"Blue" takes its title from an experimental film by gay British filmmaker Derek Jarman. The film is a blue screen with audio from Jarman and some of his favorite collaborators, a meditation on art, love, and life. It is Jarman's last film before he passed away of complications due to AIDS in 1993.

"Sweet Talk" and "Sweet Boys" are both inspired by Kara Walker's *A Subtlety, or The Marvelous Sugar Baby*. An installation in the Domino Sugar Factory, Walker's piece consisted of a monumental black, female sphinx made of a polystyrene core covered in white sugar as well as a series of attendants, black boys made of boiled sugar giving them a glossy, brown color. A commentary on sugar's role in the transatlantic slave trade, the exhibition became infamous for the ways in which white audiences interacted with the figures: taking pictures in front of the sphinx's buttocks and genitals, posing in front of her breasts, throwing up mock gang signs in front of the sugar boys, and more.

Acknowledgments

I would like to thank the editors of the following journals and anthologies where these poems first appeared (sometimes in different form):

Assaracus: "Catacombs of San Callisto," "Pass-A-Grille," "Jezebel";
Bat City Review: "O-P-U-L-E-N-C-E";
Burrow Press Review: "Bow Down," "Cedars of Lebanon";
Callaloo: "Ghost Slipper";
Columbia: A Journal of Literature and Art: "Visiting Mount Calvary Cemetery";
Connotation Press: An Online Artifact: "Sans Souci," "City of Rivers," "Heaven and Earth";
Four Way Review: "Tidewater Psalm," "Persian Blue";
Image: A Journal of Arts and Religion: "Byzantine Gold";
Kin Poetry Journal: "Sleeping Alone," "Dominion," "St. Sebastian's Executioner";
Memorious: "Cathedral," "Effigy Without a Body";
Muzzle: "Apology";
New England Review: "Okaloosa";
Nepantla: "Major Arcana: Judgment";
Nimrod: "At the Grave of Nora Neale Hurston";
OCHO: "Vespers," "We're Standing on the Sun," "Antaeus";
The Paris-American: "Sweet Boys";
Puerto Del Sol: "Illumination," "Blue," "Little Gospels," "No Union," "Primer for Sainthood";
The Queer South: Essays and Poems (Sibling Rivalry Press): "Canaan," "Breakwater";
SiDEKiCK LIT: "Fountain Statue";
Southern Humanities Review: "Sweet Talk";
Tidal Basin Review: "Devotions," "St. Mathew's Pentecostal Church";
Unsplendid: "Blaxploitation";
Waccamaw: "Summertime."

"Byzantine Gold" and "Vespers" were reprinted in *Between Midnight and Dawn: A Literary Guide to Prayer for Lent, Holy Week, and Eastertide* (Paraclete Press).

"Vespers" was translated into Spanish by Marcelo Hernandez Castillo for *Mexico City Lit*.

"Cedars of Lebanon" was included in *Best American Poetry 2015*.

"St. Mathew's Pentecostal Church" won the 2011 *Tidal Basin Review* Editorial Prize.

Many of these poems were included in a winning manuscript for a 2014 Hopwood Graduate Poetry Award from the University of Michigan.

⥽

"Blaxploitation" is for and after Erica Dawson.
"Blue" is for Eric Thomas Norris.

⥽

Thank you to the following institutions that allowed me the valuable gifts of time, space, and financial support which aided me in completing this book: The University of Tampa, The Helen Zell Writer's Program, and Cave Canem. Gratitude to my teachers at the University of Tampa: Martha Serpas, Audrey Colombe, Gianmarc Manzione, Janet Sylvester, and Erica Dawson; and at the University of Michigan: Keith Taylor, Van Jordan, Laura Kasischke, and Linda Gregerson; and to two of my earliest and best readers, Cody Waters and Laura Theobald, for their unwavering support. Thanks to my MFA cohort and Cave Canem family for their love and intellectual rigor. Girl Talk, you're my rock. Black Excellence, you're my everything. Abiding love to Lauren Clark, Marcelo Hernandez Castillo, Rubi Hernandez, Rachel Harkai, JD Duval, Lorraine Coulter, David Hornibrook, Rob Bruno, Suzi F. Garcia, Mairead Small Staid, Nate Marshall, Jeremiah Childers, Airea D. Matthews, Tina Richardson, Phillip B. Williams, Jericho Brown, L. Lamar Wilson, C. Dale Young, and Lyrae Van Clief-Stefanon. Thank you to the wonderful people at BOA for making this journey from manuscript to book such a smooth and pleasurable experience, particularly Peter Conners and Jenna Fisher. Mary Szybist, I will forever be grateful to you for seeing the light in my book and wanting to share it with the world.

⥽

About the Author

Derrick Austin is a Cave Canem fellow and earned his MFA from the University of Michigan where he was awarded a Hopwood Award in graduate poetry. His work has appeared or is forthcoming in *The Best American Poetry 2015*, *Image: A Journal of Arts and Religion*, *New England Review*, *Callaloo*, *Crab Orchard Review*, *The Paris-American*, *Memorious*, and other journals and anthologies. He lives in Ann Arbor, Michigan, where he works as the Social Media Coordinator for *The Offing*.

BOA Editions, Ltd.
The A. Poulin, Jr. New Poets of America Series

No. 1 *Cedarhome*
Poems by Barton Sutter
Foreword by W. D. Snodgrass

No. 2 *Beast Is a Wolf with Brown Fire*
Poems by Barry Wallenstein
Foreword by M. L. Rosenthal

No. 3 *Along the Dark Shore*
Poems by Edward Byrne
Foreword by John Ashbery

No. 4 *Anchor Dragging*
Poems by Anthony Piccione
Foreword by Archibald MacLeish

No. 5 *Eggs in the Lake*
Poems by Daniela Gioseffi
Foreword by John Logan

No. 6 *Moving the House*
Poems by Ingrid Wendt
Foreword by William Stafford

No. 7 *Whomp and Moonshiver*
Poems by Thomas Whitbread
Foreword by Richard Wilbur

No. 8 *Where We Live*
Poems by Peter Makuck
Foreword by Louis Simpson

No. 9 *Rose*
Poems by Li-Young Lee
Foreword by Gerald Stern

No. 10 *Genesis*
Poems by Emanuel di Pasquale
Foreword by X. J. Kennedy

No. 11 *Borders*
Poems by Mary Crow
Foreword by David Ignatow

No. 12 *Awake*
Poems by Dorianne Laux
Foreword by Philip Levine

No. 13 *Hurricane Walk*
Poems by Diann Blakely Shoaf
Foreword by William Matthews

No. 14 *The Philosopher's Club*
Poems by Kim Addonizio
Foreword by Gerald Stern

No. 15 *Bell 8*
Poems by Rick Lyon
Foreword by C. K. Williams

No. 16 *Bruise Theory*
Poems by Natalie Kenvin
Foreword by Carolyn Forché

No. 17 *Shattering Air*
Poems by David Biespiel
Foreword by Stanley Plumly

No. 18 *The Hour Between Dog and Wolf*
Poems by Laure-Anne Bosselaar
Foreword by Charles Simic

No. 19 *News of Home*
Poems by Debra Kang Dean
Foreword by Colette Inez

No. 20 *Meteorology*
Poems by Alpay Ulku
Foreword by Yusef Komunyakaa

No. 21 *The Daughters of Discordia*
Poems by Suzanne Owens
Foreword by Denise Duhamel

No. 22 *Rare Earths*
Poems by Deena Linett
Foreword by Molly Peacock

No. 23 *An Unkindness of Ravens*
Poems by Meg Kearney
Foreword by Donald Hall

No. 24 *Hunting Down the Monk*
Poems by Adrie Kusserow
Foreword by Karen Swenson

No. 25 *Big Back Yard*
Poems by Michael Teig
Foreword by Stephen Dobyns

No. 26 *Elegy with a Glass of Whiskey*
Poems by Crystal Bacon
Foreword by Stephen Dunn

Colophon

BOA Editions, Ltd., a not-for-profit publisher of poetry and other literary works, fosters readership and appreciation of contemporary literature. By identifying, cultivating, and publishing both new and established poets and selecting authors of unique literary talent, BOA brings high-quality literature to the public. Support for this effort comes from the sale of its publications, grant funding, and private donations.

The publication of this book is made possible, in part, by the special support of the following individuals:

Anonymous x 3
Nin Andrews
Angela Bonazinga & Catherine Lewis
Nickole Brown & Jessica Jacobs
Bernadette Catalana
Christopher & DeAnna Cebula
Gwen & Gary Conners
Anne C. Coon & Craig J. Zicari
Gouvernet Arts Fund
Michael Hall, *in memory of Lorna Hall*
Grant Holcomb
Christopher Kennedy & Mi Ditmar
X. J. & Dorothy M. Kennedy
Keetje Kuipers & Sarah Fritsch, *in memory of JoAnn Wood Graham*
Jack & Gail Langerak
Daniel M. Meyers, *in honor of James Shepard Skiff*
Boo Poulin
Deborah Ronnen & Sherman Levey
Steven O. Russell & Phyllis Rifkin-Russell
Sue S. Stewart, *in memory of Stephen L. Raymond*
Lynda & George Waldrep
Michael Waters & Mihaela Moscaliuc
Michael & Patricia Wilder